Writing Performance Counts

Evaluate Your Writing

. . . and Prepare for Writing Assessment

Acknowledgments
Product Development: Kent Publishing Services, Inc.
Design and Production: Signature Design Group, Inc.
Illustrations: 4, 5, N. Jo Tufts
Photos: 25, Peter Johnson/Corbis; 26, Dan Guravich/Corbis; 43, Michael & Patricia Fogdon/Corbis; 53, Michael & Patricia Fogdon/Corbis; 55, Gary Braasch/Corbis; 76, Lynn Goldsmith/Corbis; 84, Lynn Goldmsith/Corbis

ISBN: 1-56936-786-8
Options Publishing, Inc.
P.O. Box 1749
Merrimack, NH 03054-1749
TOLL FREE: 800-782-7300 • FAX: 603-424-4056
www.optionspublishing.com

All Rights Reserved. Printed in USA.
15 14 13 12 11 10 9 8 7 6 5 4 3

Table of Contents

Unit 1: Writing to Respond to Literature

Lesson 1   Think and Read 4
Lesson 2   Prewriting and Referencing 6
Lesson 3   Composing and Revising 12
Lesson 4   Editing 18
Lesson 5   Evaluate Writing 24
Lesson 6   Your Turn to Write 32

Unit 2: Writing to Persuade

Lesson 1   Think and Read 40
Lesson 2   Prewriting and Referencing 42
Lesson 3   Composing and Revising 48
Lesson 4   Editing 54
Lesson 5   Evaluate Writing 60
Lesson 6   Your Turn to Write 68

Unit 3: Writing to Explain and Inform

Lesson 1   Think and Read 76
Lesson 2   Prewriting and Referencing 78
Lesson 3   Composing and Revising 84
Lesson 4   Editing 90
Lesson 5   Evaluate Writing 96
Lesson 6   Your Turn to Write 104

Unit 1: Writing to Respond to Literature

Lesson 1

Think and Read

➤ **Can enemies become friends? That happened once to a horse and a kangaroo. On the lines below, write what you think horses and kangaroos have in common. Then read this folk tale to find out what happened when these two met.**

_____

_____

The Kangahorse

Once, long ago, a horse lived in Australia. All day long, the horse nibbled grass on a cliff overlooking the ocean.

One day while the horse was munching away, a kangaroo jumped by. The kangaroo started eating the freshest, sweetest grass in the field. The horse got very angry.

"What are you doing?" demanded the horse. "This is my grass."

"Well, don't go bananas!" said the kangaroo. "A gal has got to eat!"

"Not here!" With that, the horse put his head down and charged the kangaroo, knocking her head over heels.

The kangaroo jumped right up and gave the horse a hard kick. Soon the kangaroo and the horse were rolling on the ground wrestling. They rolled right off the cliff and into the ocean! They were so angry that they kept wrestling on the sandy ocean bottom.

Soon, a shadow passed over them. They looked up. A huge shark was circling in the water above. They quickly stopped fighting.

"Look at that shark!" said the kangaroo. "We've got to hide!"

"But where?" said the horse. "We're both so big!" Just then, an electric eel swam by.

"Hey, friend!" called the kangaroo. "Can you help us hide?"

The eel smiled. "I can help if you stand really close together."

The horse and the kangaroo hugged each other, forgetting all about their fight. Then, the eel zapped them with a bolt of electricity, melting the horse and the kangaroo together. Now, they had one body with a horse's head. This new animal looked down at itself. "At least I've still got my pocket in front!" said the kangaroo's voice.

"The shark can't see us now," the horse whispered. Their new small body was the same color as the brown seaweed, so they blended right in. Soon, the shark swam away. The horse and kangaroo took one big sigh of relief. Now they could become two again.

"Hey, Eel! You can change us back now," the kangaroo's voice yelled.

But the eel was gone. The kangaroo and the horse were joined forever. At first, this new animal was called a "kangahorse." But that was hard to say. Soon, it was called a seahorse— and it has been a seahorse ever since.

➤ Sonia's class was asked to write their own folk tales. She decided to write a folk tale about kangaroos. Before she could start writing, she needed to learn more about them.

First, Sonia wrote down several topics related to kangaroos. Then she organized her ideas into the outline below. Use the outline to answer questions 1-3.

Kangaroos
  I.   What do they look like?
  II. Where do they live?
  III.
  IV. How far can they jump?
  V.   Why do they have pockets in front?
  VI. What other animals have pockets?
  VII. Are kangaroos endangered?

1. Which of these ideas would fit BEST in the outline as section III.?

   Ⓐ Where is Australia?   Ⓒ What other animals live in Australia?
   Ⓑ What do kangaroos eat?   Ⓓ Are rabbits related to kangaroos?

2. Which of these ideas does NOT belong in Sonia's outline?

   Ⓐ II.   Ⓒ V.
   Ⓑ IV.   Ⓓ VI.

3. This outline does not include all the information that Sonia needs. What else could she find out about kangaroos?

   _____

   _____

➤ **Sonia typed the word *kangaroo* into the computer for an Internet search. Here are some of the Web sites that she found. Use Sonia's search results to answer questions 4-6.**

MATCHING SITES (1-3 of 805)

1. <u>Kangaroos</u>
   A kangaroo is a marsupial…
   www.flstate.kangaroo.edu
2. <u>Red Kangaroo Software</u>
   The best in software from
   Australia…
   www.rksoftware.com
3. <u>Kangaroos</u>
   I have always loved kangaroos…
   www.janeroberts.com

Writer's Tip

Before you begin writing:
• Brainstorm ideas for possible topics.
• List what you know about the topic you chose.
• Find reference sources for more information you can use.

4. **Which Web site seems like the best source of factual information about kangaroos?**

   Ⓐ 1   Ⓒ 3
   Ⓑ 2   Ⓓ none

5. **Which Web site probably tells one person's opinions about kangaroos?**

   Ⓐ 1   Ⓒ 3
   Ⓑ 2   Ⓓ none

6. **Which Web site has nothing to do with kangaroos?**

   Ⓐ 1   Ⓒ 3
   Ⓑ 2   Ⓓ none

Noodle Around

Writers brainstorm ideas about their topic. They write down as many ideas as they can think of. Which questions help Sonia brainstorm new ideas? Discuss your answer with a friend.

Lesson 2: Prewriting and Referencing

➤ **Now check your answers. If you answered a question incorrectly, study the correct answer.**

1. **Which of these ideas would fit BEST in the outline as section III.?**

   Answer Ⓑ is the best choice. The other answers are slightly off the topic of kangaroos.

2. **Which of these ideas does NOT belong in Sonia's outline?**

   Answer Ⓓ is correct. Sonia wants to learn about kangaroos, not all animals with pockets.

3. **This outline does not include all the information that Sonia needs. What else could she find out about kangaroos?**

   Your answers should relate to kangaroos. For example:

   What are kangaroo babies called? Do people eat kangaroo meat? Do they keep kangaroos on farms, like cows? Do kangaroos ever cause problems?

4. **Which Web site seems like the BEST source of factual information about kangaroos?**

   Answer Ⓐ is correct. The *edu* in the address for the Web site means "educational." This information comes from a school.

5. **Which Web site probably tells one person's opinions about kangaroos?**

   Answer Ⓒ is correct. The word *I* suggests that the Web site is from one person.

6. **Which Web site has nothing to do with kangaroos?**

   Answer Ⓑ is correct. This Web site sells software that happens to be named *Red Kangaroo*.

➤ **Here is a chance to work on your prewriting and referencing skills. Answer the questions on the next three pages.**

1. Writing a folk tale requires research. Which topics in Sonia's outline did the writer have to know something about in order to write "The Kangahorse"?

   _____

   _____

   _____

   _____

2. Do not limit your research to one source. Where else could Sonia have looked to find information about kangaroos? List other sources she could check.

   _____

   _____

   _____

   _____

Writer's Tip

Web sites do not always have correct information. Be sure your site has current and accurate information.

3. **Carefully choose your Web sites. Explain if these two Web sites are good sources of facts about kangaroos.**

Tipton Kangaroo rat profile
This seed-eating rodent…
www.rodent.com

_____

_____

"The Sing-Song Man of Old Kangaroo" by Rudyard Kipling
Read Kipling's tale of how the kangaroo came to look as it does now.
www.justso.com

_____

_____

4. **A folk tale is a made-up story. Would you expect Sonia to use all the information in her outline in her folk tale? Explain your answer.**

_____

_____

5. **Consider the sources of the facts you use. A classmate told Sonia that *kangaroo* means "I don't understand." Should she include this information in her folk tale? Why or why not?**

_____

_____

6. Stories should have interesting characters. As Sonia plans her folk tale, she must decide what her kangaroo is like. For example, will the kangaroo be polite or rude? Will he or she be neat or messy? Write five adjectives that Sonia might use to describe the kangaroo.

_____

_____

_____

7. In a story, the main character should solve a problem. Sonia must think of a problem for her kangaroo to solve. Think of three possible problems a kangaroo might face. Write them on the lines.

_____

_____

_____

Writer's Tip

In some ways, writing a story is like telling a story out loud. As you write, pretend you are talking to some friends.

8. Every story must have a setting. The setting describes the place and time something took place. Sonia must decide on a setting for her folk tale. Write three possible settings on the lines below.

_____

_____

_____

_____

▶ **Read the first part of Sonia's rough draft of her folk tale. Then answer questions 1-6.**

(1) Kangaroos did not always look the way they do now. (2) Long ago, they looked more like dogs or cats. (3) Long ago, Australia looked different too. (4) It was covered with thick bushes. (5) All their legs were the same size.

(6) One day, a kangaroo named Glenda was hungry. (7) She took her baby to a big field to eat grass. (8) The bushes in the field were very high. (9) I do not know what they were called. (10) Even Glenda could not see over them. (11) Then Glenda met Mona. (12) Mona is another kangaroo. (13) Mona came to the field every day. (14) Glenda and Mona talked and talked. (15) Baby kangaroos are called joeys. (16) Suddenly, Glenda could not find her joey!

1. Which sentence states the topic of this folk tale?

Ⓐ sentence 1

Ⓑ sentence 3

Ⓒ sentence 6

Ⓓ sentence 15

2. Sentence 5 is out of order. Which of these sentences would it best follow?

    Ⓐ sentence 2   Ⓒ sentence 6

    Ⓑ sentence 3   Ⓓ sentence 7

3. Which sentence below should be taken out of this story?

    Ⓐ sentence 7   Ⓒ sentence 9

    Ⓑ sentence 8   Ⓓ sentence 10

Why would you delete this sentence?

_____

_____

Writer's Tip

Put the information you have gathered into your own words. Then read it to decide if your writing says what you mean.

4. Which sentence does not add important information to the story?

    Ⓐ sentence 4   Ⓒ sentence 10

    Ⓑ sentence 7   Ⓓ sentence 13

5. Sentences 11 and 12 could be combined into one sentence. Write a new sentence for Sonia.

_____

_____

_____

6. Sentence 15 is also out of order. Which of these sentences would it best follow?

    Ⓐ sentence 6   Ⓒ sentence 8

    Ⓑ sentence 7   Ⓓ sentence 9

Noodle Around

A topic sentence not only names the subject, it also explains what readers will learn about that subject. Which question asks you about the topic sentence? Discuss with a friend whether or not Sonia wrote a good topic sentence.

➤ **Now check your answers. If you answered a question incorrectly, study the correct answer.**

1. **Which sentence states the topic of this folk tale?**

   Answer Ⓐ is correct. Sentence 1 introduces the topic of the folk tale—kangaroos look different now. All the other sentences explain details.

2. **Sentence 5 is out of order. Which of these sentences would it best follow?**

   Answer Ⓐ is correct. Sentence 2 begins to explain how kangaroos looked long ago. Sentence 5 adds more details.

3. **Which sentence below should be taken out of this story? Why would you delete this sentence?**

   Answer Ⓒ is correct. Whether Sonia does or does not know the name of the bushes is not important to the story.

4. **Which sentence does not add important information to the story?**

   Answer Ⓓ is correct. It is not important that Mona came to the field every day. The other answers add important details to the story.

5. **Sentences 11 and 12 could be combined into one sentence. Write a new sentence for Sonia.**

   Your rewrite should not change the meaning of the sentence. For example: Then Glenda met Mona, another kangaroo.

6. **Sentence 15 is also out of order. Which of these sentences would it best follow?**

   Answer Ⓑ is correct. Sentence 7 is the first time the baby is mentioned. Sentence 15 should come next, to explain what baby kangaroos are called.

➤ **Here is a chance to work on your composing and revising skills. Answer the questions on the next three pages.**

1. **Do not repeat yourself in your writing. Which sentence below repeats information that Sonia has already explained?**

   Ⓐ Long ago, kangaroos did not have big back legs.

   Ⓑ Glenda and Mona were good friends.

   Ⓒ Most kangaroos live in Australia.

   Ⓓ Mona joined Glenda in the field every day.

2. **When you write stories, include only details and facts that add important information. Which sentence below would add important information to Sonia's folk tale? Explain your choice.**

   Ⓐ The joey jumped out of Glenda's pouch and started eating the grass.

   Ⓑ Joey is also a boy's name.

   _____

   _____

3. **A topic sentence tells what a paragraph or a story is about. How do you know that sentence 3 is not the topic of this folk tale?**

   _____

   _____

   _____

4. **Short, choppy sentences sound awkward. Combine sentences 3 and 4 on page 12 into one sentence. Do not change the meaning of the sentences.**

_____

_____

_____

5. **Carefully choose the details you include. Which of the sentences below should Sonia add to her story? Explain your answer.**

   Ⓐ Only female kangaroos have pouches.
   Ⓑ Mona and Glenda were good friends.

_____

_____

6. **Put your sentences in a logical order. Sonia wants to add the sentence below to her story. Which sentence in the story should it follow? Why?**

   Glenda became very worried.

_____

_____

7. **Descriptive words and phrases can help readers see what you mean. Rewrite sentence 7 on page 12 to tell readers what the field looked like. Add at least two descriptive words or phrases.**

_____

_____

8. **Each paragraph should contain one main idea. Sonia has decided that her second paragraph on page 12 is too long. Which sentence should begin a new third paragraph? Explain your answer.**

_____

_____

9. **Which choice below is NOT a run-on?**

Ⓐ Suddenly, Glenda could not find her joey, he had disappeared!
Ⓑ Suddenly, Glenda could not find her joey. He had disappeared!
Ⓒ Suddenly, Glenda could not find her joey he had disappeared!

10. **Also avoid sentence fragments. Rewrite the fragment below so that Sonia can add it to her story.**

Sweet grass under the thick bushes.

_____

_____

Writer's Tip

As you write your first draft, don't worry about spelling errors. Try and get your thoughts down on paper first.

➤ **Read the end of Sonia's rough draft of her folk tale. This section has groups of underlined words. Editing questions will be asked about them.**

(17) Glenda and Mona looked all around for the baby kangaroo, or joey. (18) They could not see very far because the bushes were <u>to thick</u>. (19) Glenda became very <u>frightned</u>. (20) She began jumping as high as she could. (21) <u>She try</u> to see over the tall bushes. (22) As she jumped, her back legs got <u>strongest and strongest</u>.

(23) "<u>Look!</u> Mona said. (24) "Your back legs are bigger now!" (25) Glenda's back legs were now so big and strong that she could jump high in the air. (26) With one more big jump, she finally <u>seen</u> her joey and hurried to get him. (27) When the other kangaroos heard what happened, they started jumping, too. (28) Soon all the kangaroos had <u>big, strong, powerful</u> back legs, just like they do today!

1. **What is the mistake in the underlined part of sentence 18? How should Sonia edit it?**

   _____

   _____

2. **How should Sonia edit the underlined word in sentence 19?**

   Ⓐ frigtened   Ⓒ frightened

   Ⓑ freightened   Ⓓ no change needed

3. How should Sonia edit the underlined part of sentence 21?

Ⓐ She trying   Ⓒ She tried

Ⓑ She tryed   Ⓓ no change needed

4. How should Sonia edit the underlined part of sentence 22? Rewrite the sentence for her.

_____

_____

5. How should Sonia edit the underlined part of sentence 23?

Ⓐ "Look"   Ⓒ "look!"

Ⓑ "Look!"   Ⓓ no change needed

6. How should Sonia edit the underlined part of sentence 26?

Ⓐ seed   Ⓒ seeing

Ⓑ saw   Ⓓ no change needed

7. How should Sonia edit the underlined part of sentence 28?

Ⓐ big, strong, and, powerful

Ⓑ big, strong and, powerful

Ⓒ big, strong, and powerful

Ⓓ no change needed

Writer's Tip

When you edit, make sure you:
- capitalize the correct words
- spell all words correctly
- use homonyms correctly, such as hear (not here) to mean "listen"
- use punctuation marks in the correct places.

Noodle Around

Homonyms are words that sound the same but have different spellings. Which question asks you about homonyms? With a buddy, list as many homonyms as you can.

Lesson 4: Editing

➤ **Now check your answers. If you answered a question incorrectly, find out why another answer is correct.**

1. **What is the mistake in the underlined part of sentence 18? How should Sonia edit it?**

   It should be *too thick*. *To* is a preposition. *Two* is the number 2. *Too* means also. *Too* is also an adjective or an adverb.

2. **How should Sonia edit the underlined word in sentence 19?**

   Answer Ⓒ is the correct spelling of this word.

3. **How should Sonia edit the underlined part of sentence 21?**

   Answer Ⓒ is correct. The verb should be in past tense to match the other verbs in the story. Change the *y* to *i* before adding *-ed*.

4. **How should Sonia edit the underlined part of sentence 22?**

   Sonia is comparing two things—the way Glenda's legs are and the way they used to be. She should use the ending *-er*: For example:
   As she jumped, her back legs got stronger and stronger.

5. **How should Sonia edit the underlined part of sentence 23?**

   Answer Ⓑ is correctly punctuated. Mona's speech should have quotation marks before and after it. The word should also be capitalized.

6. **How should Sonia edit the underlined part of sentence 26?**

   Answer Ⓑ is the right one. *Saw* is in the past tense, like the other verbs in this story. It is also spelled correctly.

7. **How should Sonia edit the underlined part of sentence 28?**

   Answer Ⓒ is correct. Sonia should place a comma before the word *and*.

➤ **Here is a chance to practice your editing skills. Answer the questions on the next three pages.**

1. **Some words sound the same but have very different spellings and meanings. Be careful to use the correct spelling. Each sentence below uses the word *to, too,* or *two.* Write *C* for correct or *I* for incorrect before each sentence.**

   a. _____ Glenda could not see when she tried too look over the bushes.

   b. _____ She jumped up in the air two more times.

   c. _____ The bushes were just to high.

   d. _____ They were very thick, too.

2. **When a verb ends in a consonant and *-y,* change the *y* to *i* before adding the ending. When it ends in a vowel and *-y,* just add the ending. Write the past tense of each verb below.**

   a. cry _____   **d.** dry _____

   b. play _____   **e.** enjoy_____

   c. destroy_____   **f.** stay_____

3. **We use the ending *-er* to compare two things and the ending *-est* to compare more than two things. Circle the word that correctly completes each sentence below.**

   a. The kangaroo's front legs are (smaller / smallest) than its back legs.

   b. Are kangaroos the (larger / largest) native animals in Australia?

   c. As the joey gets (bigger / biggest), it can no longer fit in its mother's pouch.

   d. The oldest joey is the (taller / tallest) of all the joeys.

Lesson 4: Editing

4. Irregular verbs such as *see* do not add *-ed* to form the past tense. *Saw* is the past tense of *see*. Write the past tense of these irregular verbs.

a. bring _____

c. make _____

b. go _____

d. say _____

5. Homonyms are words that sound the same but have different spellings and meanings. Circle the correct spelling in each sentence below.

a. They should be (hear / here) soon.

b. I can (hear / here) them coming.

c. (They're / There / Their) almost here!

d. I can hear (they're / there / their) voices.

e. (They're / There / Their) they are!

6. To form the past tense of some verbs, you must change the spelling. In each sentence below, circle the correct spelling of the past tense verb.

a. Glenda (came / comed) to the field every day.

b. She (worried / worryed) about her joey.

c. The joey (finded / found) some sweet grass to eat.

d. Glenda (hurryed / hurried) to find him.

7. Use the *-er* ending when you are comparing two things and using short words. Use the word *more* when you compare two things using longer words. Write *C* for correct or *I* for incorrect next to each sentence.

a. _____ Glenda's back legs grew more big.

b. _____ They were more powerful than before.

c. _____ Now she could jump higher.

d. _____ All the other kangaroos wanted to be more strong, too.

8. Use the *-est* ending when you are comparing three or more things using short words. Use the word *most* when you compare three or more things using longer words. Underline the correct form in each sentence.

   a. For a while, Glenda was the (most tall / tallest) kangaroo in Australia.

   b. The kangaroos had a contest to see who could jump the (most high / highest).

   c. I think kangaroos are the (most unusual / unusualest) animals.

   d. Are they the (most interesting / interestingest) of all animals?

9. Use quotation marks around a speaker's exact words. Each sentence below includes quotation marks. Write *C* for correct and *I* for incorrect next to each sentence.

   a. _____ Glenda asked, Did you see my joey?"

   b. _____ Mona said, "No, I have not seen him."

   c. _____ "Where do you think he went? Glenda asked.

10. Use commas to separate three or more words in a series. Write *C* for correct or *I* for incorrect next to each sentence.

    a. _____ Mona, and Glenda's joey nibbled on the grass.

    b. _____ Glenda, and her baby were hungry.

    c. _____ Glenda looked north, south, east, and west for her joey.

Writer's Tip

Many people enjoy reading make-believe stories, but hardly anyone enjoys reading "make-believe" spelling. Check to make sure you correct your spelling errors.

Lesson 4: Editing

➤ **Now you are going to read and evaluate a folk tale that Miki wrote. It is about animals that started out as enemies and became friends. He needs you to help make his writing better. Before you begin, read the checklist below.**

Writing Checklist

Miki will earn his best score if he meets these goals:

Ideas	• Excellent ideas
Order	• Ideas are in order
Sentences	• Sentences are easy to understand
Spelling and Punctuation	• No more than two mistakes

Directions: Write a folk tale about people or animals. Explain how they were once enemies, then became friends. Use your imagination. Put the events in an order that makes sense. Think of a strong beginning, middle, and end.

A Friendship Built on Bugs

(1) Long ago, cattle did not lives on farms. (2) On huge fields called plains. (3) All day long, the cattle munched on the thick grass that grew there. (4) The cattle did not mind the other animals, but they disliked the egrets. (5) Those white, long-legged, long-necked birds were pests. (6) They were always standing right beside the cows, under there feet. (7) Other animals lived there, too. (8) There were buffalo, deer, and rabbits.

(9) The cattle tried to get rid of the egrets. (10) The egrets were brilliant white in color. (11) They yelled, "Get out of here, you pests!" (12) Still, the birds were always there, standing too close to the cows. (13) They would peck, peck, peck at the grass that the cattle were trying to eat.

(14) "How can we get rid of those birds?" the cattle asked each other.

(15) The cattle had noticed that the birds not like to be bumped. (16) The egrets would squawk and fly into the air a little ways. (17) Soon, though, they would be back under the cattle's feet, pecking away. (18) The cattle decided to keep bumping into the egrets. (19) They hoped the birds would leave them alone.

(20) It worked! (21) After several days of getting pushed around, the birds left. (22) The cattle did not know where they went, they did not care. (23) Now they could walk anywhere they wanted without those egrets getting in the way.

(24) However, now the cattle were itchy because bugs bit them all day long. (25) "Where did all these bugs come from?" they asked each other. (26) Then they knew! (27) The bugs where there because the egrets were not eating them anymore!

(28) The cattle searched until they finded the egrets. (29) "please come back and live with us again" the cattle begged. (30) "We need you!"

(31)"Will you keep pushing us around?" asked the birds.

(32) "Never!" the cattle promised. (33) "You will be our special guests!"

➤ **Now answer the following questions about Miki's folk tale.**

1. **Sentence 1 has a mistake in it. Rewrite the sentence correctly.**

   _____

   _____

2. **Sentence 6 has a word that is used incorrectly. Which word below would you would use in place of this word?**

   Ⓐ rite   Ⓒ their

   Ⓑ besides   Ⓓ they're

3. **Sentences 7 and 8 are not in the correct place. Which one of these sentences should they follow?**

   Ⓐ sentence 1   Ⓒ sentence 4

   Ⓑ sentence 3   Ⓓ sentence 5

4. **Which of these sentences could be taken out of the folk tale?**

   Ⓐ sentence 9

   Ⓑ sentence 10

   Ⓒ sentence 11

   Ⓓ sentence 12

   Why would you take it out?

   _____

   _____

Writer's Tip

Do certain words such as *there, their,* and *they're* give you problems? Write a set of sentences that use each word correctly. Keep them in a journal for future reference.

5. **Miki left a word out of sentence 15. Rewrite the sentence, adding the important missing word.**

_____

_____

_____

6. **Which sentence on page 25 is a fragment?**

Ⓐ sentence 2

Ⓑ sentence 6

Ⓒ sentence 9

Ⓓ sentence 11

Writer's Tip

Careless mistakes are easy to sea. (Did you notice the mistake in that sentence?) Careful proofreading helps readers enjoy your story, not your mistakes.

7. **Which sentence on page 26 is a run-on sentence?**

Ⓐ sentence 19   Ⓒ sentence 21

Ⓑ sentence 20   Ⓓ sentence 22

8. **Miki used the wrong word in sentence 27. Which word below should be used instead of this incorrect word?**

Ⓐ were   Ⓒ it

Ⓑ their   Ⓓ any more

9. **Sentence 28 has a mistake in it. Rewrite it correctly.**

_____

_____

©2001 Options Publishing, Inc.

10. Sentence 29 is incorrectly punctuated. Which sentence below is correct?

Ⓐ "Please come back and live with us again" the cattle begged.

Ⓑ "Please come back and live with us again, the cattle begged.

Ⓒ "Please come back and live with us again," the cattle begged.

Ⓓ "please come back and live with us again," the cattle begged.

11. Miki did not describe the cattle in his folk tale very well. Write several words and phrases that would give the reader a better description.

_____

_____

_____

12. A closing paragraph tells what happens at the end of the story. Miki has not written a closing paragraph. Write one for him. You will have to decide if the egrets decided to move back with the cattle or not.

_____

_____

_____

_____

_____

_____

Writer's Tip

Interesting writing requires interesting words. Miki used *munched* to describe how the cattle ate. He called the cattle *itchy* instead of *uncomfortable*. *Munched* and *itchy* help readers picture the cattle.

Lesson 5: Evaluate Writing

➤ **Here is a guide for evaluating writing. It is called a rubric (rhymes with *picnic*). Rubrics are used to grade writing tests. Use this rubric to evaluate Miki's folk tale.**

Writing Rubric

Score	Ideas	Order	Sentences	Spelling and Punctuation
4	• Excellent ideas	• Ideas are in order	• Sentences are easy to understand	• No more than two mistakes
3	• Good ideas	• Most ideas are in order	• Most sentences are easy to understand	• No more than four mistakes
2	• Some ideas are not about the subject	• Some ideas are in order	• Some sentences are easy to understand	• No more than six mistakes
1	• Most ideas are not about the subject	• Few ideas are in order	• Few sentences are easy to understand	• No more than eight mistakes
0	• No work done	• No work done	• No work done	• No work done

➤ Give Miki's writing a score of 0 to 4 for each category. Explain why you gave him that score.

Ideas _____

score

_____

_____

Order _____

score

_____

_____

Sentences _____

score

_____

_____

Spelling and Punctuation _____

score

_____

_____

Lesson 5: Evaluate Writing

> **Read the directions below. Then, read the checklist that you and your teacher will use to evaluate your writing.**

Directions: Now it is your turn to write a folk tale. First, think of an unusual animal. Then make up a folk tale about something the animal did. In folk tales, animals can talk. Other strange things can also happen.

Make sure your folk tale is well organized. Think of a strong beginning, middle, and end. Use descriptive words to make your characters and setting seem real.

Writing Checklist

I will earn my best score if I achieve the following:

Ideas	• Excellent ideas
Order	• Ideas are in order
Sentences	• Sentences are easy to understand
Spelling and Punctuation	• No more than two mistakes

Plan Your Writing

➤ **Use these pages to plan your writing. You might find this graphic organizer helpful.**

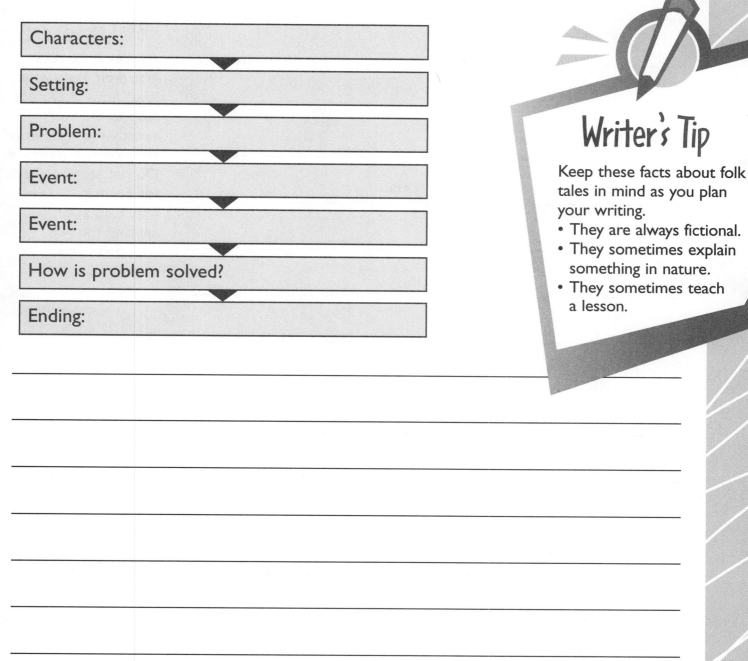

Characters:

Setting:

Problem:

Event:

Event:

How is problem solved?

Ending:

Writer's Tip

Keep these facts about folk tales in mind as you plan your writing.
- They are always fictional.
- They sometimes explain something in nature.
- They sometimes teach a lesson.

_____

_____

_____

_____

_____

_____

_____

Plan Your Writing

_____

_____

_____

_____

_____

_____

_____

Writer's Tip

As you write, ask yourself whether each fact, event, or comment is important to the story. If not, leave it out.

_____

_____

_____

Writer's Tip

Exchange your writing with a partner. You will be able to find places for improvement in each other's work more easily than you can find them in your own story.

_____

_____

_____

Lesson 6: Your Turn to Write

Write Your Final Draft

➤ **Use all the skills you have learned in this unit to score well on a final draft. Remember to carefully proofread your work before you give it to your teacher.**

1 _____

2 _____

3 _____

4 _____

5 _____

6 _____

7 _____

8 _____

9 _____

10 _____

11 _____

12 _____

13 _____

14 _____

15 _____

16 _____

17 _____

18 _____

19 _____

20 _____

21 _____

22 _____

23 _____

24 _____

25 _____

26 _____

27 _____

28 _____

29 _____

30 _____

31 _____

32 _____

33 _____

Lesson 6: Your Turn to Write

➤ **Here is the same rubric you used to evaluate Miki's folk tale. Now use it to evaluate your own folk tale.**

Writing Rubric

Score	Ideas	Order	Sentences	Spelling and Punctuation
4	• Excellent ideas	• Ideas are in order	• Sentences are easy to understand	• No more than two mistakes
3	• Good ideas	• Most ideas are in order	• Most sentences are easy to understand	• No more than four mistakes
2	• Some ideas are not about the subject	• Some ideas are in order	• Some sentences are easy to understand	• No more than six mistakes
1	• Most ideas are not about the subject	• Few ideas are in order	• Few sentences are easy to understand	• No more than eight mistakes
0	• No work done	• No work done	• No work done	• No work done

➤ **Give your own writing a score of 0 to 4 for each category. Explain why you gave yourself that score.**

Ideas _____

score

_____

_____

Order _____

score

_____

_____

Sentences _____

score

_____

_____

Spelling and Punctuation _____

score

_____

_____

Lesson 1

Think and Read

➤ **Many people are trying to protect rare animals. On the lines below, name some animals that you think are important for us to save. Also name some that you think are less important. Then read this article. See if it changes your mind about which animals are important.**

_____

_____

Saving Ourselves

Save the pandas! How many times have you heard that? Of course we want to save animals that are so cute. However, many animals that are not cute also need to be saved. Why? Because people need some of these animals to save their lives.

Cute pandas like this need to be saved.

Each kind of living thing is called a species. We lose about 1,000 species every year. They are gone from Earth forever. No one kills them on purpose. Yet people do things to destroy their homes. They cut down rainforests and dump garbage into the oceans. These actions leave the animals that live in the rainforests and oceans with nowhere to live. Many die.

Why does it matter? We might be losing species that can help us. Vampire bats, for example, live by sucking blood from animals. Not many people want to protect them. Yet their spit has a special chemical in it. This chemical stops blood from clotting. Clots can stop blood from flowing to the heart and brain, causing injury or death. Doctors use this chemical to prevent blood clots in people.

Copperhead snakes are dangerous. Few people want to protect them. However, like vampire bats, they have special spit that can stop blood from clotting. A chemical in snake spit is already saving people's lives.

Most animals that live in the ocean are not cute. Mussels and slugs are two examples. Mussels look like clams. Blue mussels make glue that holds them onto rocks. Then, waves cannot carry them away. Doctors use mussel glue on people. They use it to repair teeth and to close cuts without using stitches.

Scary-looking copperhead snakes also need to be protected.

The soft, fat sea slug lives in coral reefs. It looks like a snail without a shell. The sea slug is full of chemicals that taste bad. Those chemicals stop fish from eating the slug. Now doctors have found another use for these chemicals. They can kill cancer cells in people. That is good news!

Should we save animals? Yes, but we need to try to protect them all, not just the cute ones. Who knows which species might save thousands of human lives? If we help save as many species as possible, we are also saving ourselves.

Prewriting and Referencing

➤ **Raymond's class was assigned to write a persuasive article. He decided to persuade people that vampire bats are helpful, not dangerous.**

Raymond wanted to find more information about the bats. He used a chart to organize the information he found. Use the chart to answer questions 1-2.

Topic: Vampire Bats	Details
Who first discovered them?	
What do they look like?	
What do they eat?	
When do they come out?	
Why do they have this name?	
How can vampire bats help us?	

1. **Which of these statements is the BEST detail for the topic "What do they look like?"**

   Ⓐ Many vampire bats live in caves.

   Ⓑ Vampire bats live in colonies of up to 2,000 bats.

   Ⓒ Vampire bats suck about one ounce of blood a night.

   Ⓓ Vampire bats can be gray, brown, or reddish-brown.

2. **What else could Raymond find out about vampire bats? Help him come up with more topics about vampire bats.**

   _____

   _____

➤ **Here is the index from a book about vampire bats. Use it to answer questions 3-5.**

INDEX

Vampire Bats

  Areas where they live, 13-15

  Colonies (families), 8-9

  Description, 1-4

  Diseases they carry, 17-20

  Feeding, 5-6

  Human health, 22-23

  Hunting skills, 10-12

  Kinds of bats, 6-8

  Problems they cause, 15-20

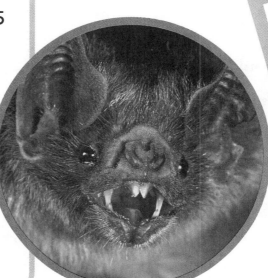

3. **Which pages would tell Raymond what vampire bats look like?**

   Ⓐ 13-15   Ⓒ 5-6

   Ⓑ 1-4   Ⓓ 15-20

4. **Which pages would explain how bat spit helps people?**

   Ⓐ 17-20   Ⓒ 22-23

   Ⓑ 5-6   Ⓓ 15-20

5. **Which pages would tell Raymond whether vampire bats live near him?**

   Ⓐ 13-15   Ⓒ 22-23

   Ⓑ 8-9   Ⓓ 10-12

Lesson 2: Prewriting and Referencing

➤ **Now check your answers. If you answered a question incorrectly, study the correct answer.**

1. **Which of these statements is the BEST detail for the topic "What do they look like?"**

   Answer Ⓓ is correct. It tells how bats look.

2. **What else could Raymond find out about vampire bats?**

   Your answer should relate closely to vampire bats. For example:

   How do these bats find their prey? Do they carry rabies or other diseases? What are their enemies?

3. **Which pages would tell Raymond what vampire bats look like?**

   Did you choose Answer Ⓑ? The word *description* means "what something looks like."

4. **Which pages would explain how bat spit helps people?**

   Answer Ⓒ is the correct choice because pages 22-23 discuss how bats affect the health of people.

5. **Where should Raymond look to find out whether vampire bats live near him?**

   Answer Ⓐ would tell him. Pages 13-15 tell where vampire bats live.

Try It

➤ **Here is a chance to work on your prewriting and referencing skills. Answer the questions on the next three pages.**

1. When you do research, you might find many facts and details. How did the chart on page 42 help Raymond?

_____

_____

2. Raymond found some facts about bats that he did not expect to find. What should he do with information that does not fit under any of the categories in his chart? Explain your answer.

_____

_____

_____

3. You must use the latest facts when writing about health. The index on page 43 is from a book published in 1992. Where could Raymond find more up-to-date information about how a chemical in bat spit helps people?

_____

_____

_____

_____

Lesson 2: Prewriting and Referencing

4. When you research a topic, keep an open mind and stay focused on your topic. Which items in the index on page 43 are not about Raymond's topic?

_____

_____

5. Raymond's chart helped him organize his facts. Which question in the chart will be most useful as he writes about his topic? Explain your answer.

_____

_____

6. The index of a book can help you find information. Which pages in the index on page 43 explain how bats find their prey?

_____

_____

7. Information is listed in a certain order in indexes. Why are the topics in this index not listed in the order they appear in the book? In what order are they listed?

_____

_____

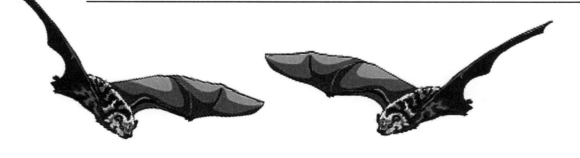

8. A table of contents can also help you find information. How is a table of contents different from an index?

_____

_____

9. When you write a persuasive article, include the most convincing facts you can find. Below are some facts that Raymond found. Which one is the most likely to convince readers that vampire bats are helpful? Explain your answer.

Ⓐ Vampire bats do not suck blood. They make a small cut and lick the blood that flows out of it.

Ⓑ A substance in vampire spit can help people avoid heart attacks.

Ⓒ Vampire bats come out only at night.

Ⓓ Vampire bats have feathery wings.

10. Make sure your report is accurate. Raymond's best friend told him bats can be used to make clothing. Raymond trusts his friend but isn't sure his friend's information is true. What should Raymond do with the information?

_____

_____

_____

_____

Writer's Tip
To convince readers of something, you must understand why they might disagree. Try to see your topic or question from the reader's point of view.

> **Read this part of Raymond's rough draft. Then answer questions 1-6.**

---

(1) Many people are afraid of vampire bats. (2) They learned about vampire bats from horror movies. (3) In these movies, vampires can change into bats. (4) Then they can sneak up on people. (5) Vampires can also change into wolves. (6) However, people should not be afraid of real vampire bats.

(7) Vampire bats live in Mexico and South America. (8) They sleep in caves all day long. (9) They also sleep in old, empty buildings. (10) They might choose a horse, a cow, a pig, or a chicken. (11) At night, they fly around looking for animals to bite.

(12) These bats have sharp front teeth, they can bite through skin. (13) One stops the animal from feeling the bite. (14) The other chemical stops the blood from clotting. (15) This keeps blood flowing from the bite. (16) Bat spit has two special chemicals in it.

---

1. **Which sentence states the main point of this persuasive article?**

   Ⓐ sentence 1   Ⓒ sentence 7

   Ⓑ sentence 6   Ⓓ sentence 12

2. **Which sentence below should be taken out of this story?**

   Ⓐ sentence 2   Ⓒ sentence 4

   Ⓑ sentence 3   Ⓓ sentence 5

3. **Sentences 8 and 9 could be combined into one sentence. Rewrite these sentences to tell about one main idea.**

_____

_____

_____

Writer's Tip

Use examples to show readers what you mean. For instance, instead of just saying that some animals help us, the article _Saving Ourselves_ includes examples of animals that help us.

4. **Sentence 10 is out of order. Which of these sentences would it best follow?**

Ⓐ sentence 6   Ⓒ sentence 8

Ⓑ sentence 7   Ⓓ sentence 11

5. **Find the sentence on page 48 that is a run-on and does not have a clear main idea. Rewrite it as two sentences to tell about two ideas.**

_____

_____

_____

Noodle Around

6. **Look back at the directions on page 42 that Raymond was given. Do you think Raymond followed the directions? Explain your answer.**

_____

_____

_____

_____

Sometimes two complete sentences are combined into one sentence. If no punctuation or joining words are used to combine the sentences, it is called a run-on. Which question asks you about a run-on sentence?

©2001 Options Publishing, Inc.

➤ **Now check your answers. If you answered a question incorrectly, study the correct answer.**

1. **Which sentence states the main point of this persuasive article?**

   Answer Ⓑ is correct. Sentence 6 explains what Raymond is trying to persuade his readers to believe.

2. **Which sentence below should be taken out of this story?**

   Answer Ⓓ is correct. Sentence 5 does not add important information.

3. **Sentences 8 and 9 could be combined into one sentence. Rewrite these sentences to tell about one main idea.**

   Your new sentence should not change the meaning. For example:

   All day long, they sleep in caves or in old, empty buildings.

4. **Sentence 10 is out of order. Which of these sentences would it best follow?**

   Answer Ⓓ is correct. Sentence 11 says the bats fly around looking for animals, and sentence 10 names the animals the bats might find.

5. **Find the sentence on page 48 that is a run-on and does not have a clear main idea. Rewrite it as two sentences to tell about two ideas.**

   Sentence 12 is a run-on. You might rewrite it in this way:

   These bats have sharp front teeth. They can quickly bite through skin.

6. **Do you think Raymond followed the directions he was given on page 42 while writing his rough draft? Explain your answer.**

   Raymond has not followed the directions. He was directed to write a pesuasive article. However, he has not stated any opinions backed up by facts about the topic yet. A good persuasion states the writer's point-of-view in the first paragraph.

©2001 Options Publishing, Inc.

➤ **Here is a chance to work on your composing and revising skills. Answer the questions on the next three pages.**

1. **A persuasive article usually begins by stating what the writer wants readers to believe. Which sentence below explains the main point of the article on pages 40 and 41? Explain your answer.**

   Ⓐ Save the pandas!

   Ⓑ We need to protect all other animals, too.

   Ⓒ Each kind of living thing is called a species.

   Ⓓ We lose about 1,000 species a year.

   _____

   _____

2. **Every sentence in an article should be closely related to the writer's main point. Which sentence below adds important information to Raymond's article? Explain why.**

   Ⓐ Bats eat many harmful insects.

   Ⓑ Mexico is part of North America.

   _____

   _____

3. **Put your sentences in a logical order. Raymond wants to add the sentence below to his article. Which sentence should it follow? Why?**
   You are not likely to see a vampire bat in the United States.

   _____

   _____

4. **Writers need to present their ideas in a logical order. The sentences below are mixed up. Number them from 1 to 4.**

   a. _____ Within the colony are smaller groups of bats.

   b. _____ A colony can have 2,000 members.

   c. _____ Vampire bats often live in large colonies.

   d. _____ One group might have ten females, one male, and many baby bats.

5. **Run-on sentences are hard to read and understand. Rewrite these run-on sentences as two complete sentences.**

   Vampire bats are very active on the ground, they have powerful hind legs.

   _____

   _____

   Vampire bats have fewer teeth than other bats, these teeth are very sharp.

   _____

   _____

6. **Make sure all of the facts relate to your topic. Which of the sentences below should Raymond add to his article? Explain your answer.**

   Ⓐ My favorite vampire movie is "The Horror of Dracula."
   Ⓑ Most bats eat insects, but vampire bats drink blood.

   _____

   _____

7. Rewrite the two short sentences below as one sentence.

Vampire bats have no tails. They can run fast and jump high.

_____

_____

8. Raymond wants to add the sentence below to his article. Rewrite it so it is clearer.

Scientists have found bats can for people be useful.

_____

_____

9. A sentence fragment is missing the subject or verb. Always write in complete sentences. Write *C* for complete or *F* for fragment next to each group of words.

a. _____ Vampire bats live in warm climates.

b. _____ Flying low over the ground.

c. _____ They look for resting animals.

d. _____ Often do not realize they have been bitten.

Writer's Tip

Make sure your writing has an interesting beginning, a clearly explained middle, and an ending that wraps everything up.

Lesson 3: Composing and Revising

➤ **Read the rest of Raymond's rough draft of his persuasive article. This section has groups of underlined words. Editing questions will be asked about them.**

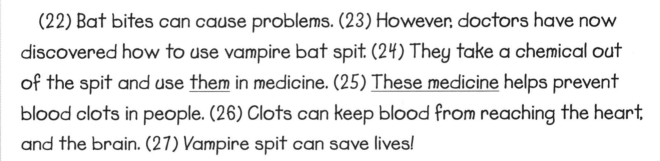

(17) A bat drinks about two tablespoons of blood each night. (18) That's about one ounce. (19) Bats weigh only about two ounces themselves!

(20) Bat bites can get infected and make animals sick. (21) Some <u>bat carry</u> rabies, a disease that can kill animals.

(22) Bat bites can cause problems. (23) However, doctors have now discovered how to use vampire bat spit. (24) They take a chemical out of the spit and use <u>them</u> in medicine. (25) <u>These medicine</u> helps prevent blood clots in people. (26) Clots can keep blood from reaching the heart, and the brain. (27) Vampire spit can save lives!

(28) Vampire bats live only in certain place. (29) They would rather bite animals than people. (30) <u>We</u> should not be afraid of them. (31) Instead, <u>you</u> should be glad they can help us stay healthy.

1. **How should Raymond edit the underlined part of sentence 21?**

   (A) bats carries   (C) bat carries

   (B) bats carry   (D) no change needed

2. **Which word below should replace the underlined word in sentence 24?**

   (A) it   (C) him

   (B) they   (D) no change needed

3. How should Raymond edit the underlined part of sentence 25?

Ⓐ This medicines

Ⓒ This medicine

Ⓑ Those medicine

Ⓓ no change needed

4. How should Raymond punctuate sentence 26? Rewrite it below with the correct punctuation.

_____

_____

Writer's Tip

Always make sure subjects agree with verbs. Singular goes with singular; plural goes with plural. For example, *The boys walk quickly past.* In this example, the subject and verb are both plural.

5. Which word in sentence 28 should end with *s*?

Ⓐ Vampire

Ⓒ place

Ⓑ live

Ⓓ no change needed

6. Rewrite sentence 31 so the underlined pronoun agrees with the underlined pronoun in sentence 30.

_____

_____

_____

Noodle Around

A noun that ends in *s* is usually plural. Which question asks you about plural nouns?

©2001 Options Publishing, Inc.

Lesson 4: Editing

➤ **Now check your answers. If you answered a question incorrectly, study the correct answer.**

1. **How should Raymond edit the underlined part of sentence 21?**

   Answer Ⓑ is correct. The subject *bats* is plural, and the verb *carry* is plural.

2. **Which word below should replace the underlined word in sentence 24?**

   Did you choose Answer Ⓐ? This pronoun must be singular to match *chemical* which is also singular.

3. **How should Raymond edit the underlined part of sentence 25?**

   Answer Ⓒ is correct because *medicine* is singular. It needs a singular pronoun such as *this*.

4. **How should Raymond punctuate sentence 26? Rewrite it below with the correct punctuation.**

   No comma is needed when only two places are mentioned.
   Clots can keep blood from reaching the heart and the brain.

5. **Which word in sentence 28 should end with *s* ?**

   Answer Ⓒ is the correct answer. *Place* should be plural. It refers to Mexico and South America—two places.

6. **Rewrite sentence 31 so the underlined pronoun agrees with the underlined pronoun in sentence 30.**

   Replace *you* with *we* in sentence 31 to match *We* in sentence 30.
   Instead, we should be glad they can help us stay healthy.
   Now *we* also matches *us* at the end of the sentence.

➤ **Here is a chance to work on your editing skills. Answer the questions on the next three pages.**

1. **Verbs must agree with subjects. Circle the correct verb in each sentence.**

   a. Vampire bats in zoos (has / have) lived more than nineteen years.

   b. A bat in a zoo (gets / get) all the food and care it needs.

   c. Bats that live in the wild (is / are) on their own.

2. **A pronoun must agree with the word it replaces or refers to. Circle each correct pronoun.**

   a. Farmers often kill bats because (it / they) harm (his / their) animals.

   b. However, a bat is helpful because (it / they) eats thousands of insects.

   c. Some people say that bats are worth (its / their) weight in gold.

3. **Pronouns must agree with the nouns they replace. Circle the correct pronoun in each sentence.**

   a. (This / These) clots can block the flow of blood.

   b. (That / Those) can lead to a heart attack or a stroke.

Writer's Tip

Some pronouns refer to a noun. A pronoun must be singular to agree with a singular noun, or plural to agree with a plural noun.

Lesson 4: Editing

4. Commas separate three or more words in a series. A comma is also used when two sentences are joined with a conjunction. Rewrite these sentences using the correct punctuation.

This chemical can prevent blood clots quickly, safely and cheaply.

_____

_____

Drug companies are always looking for new drugs and they often look in strange or unusual places.

_____

_____

5. Subjects and verbs should always agree. Check the subjects and verbs in the sentences below. Write *C* for correct or *I* for incorrect next to each sentence.

a. _____ An article about bats sound interesting to me.

b. _____ Articles about animals always get my attention.

c. _____ A colony of bats lives in my uncle's old barn.

d. _____ The bats from the colony flies around at night.

6. Pronouns must agree with the words they replace. Circle the correct pronoun in each sentence.

a. If bat bites become infected, (it / they) can make animals sick.

b. If a bat bit you, do you think you would feel (it / them)?

c. A bat bites with (its / their) extra-sharp front teeth.

d. Farmers must carefully check (its / their) animals for bat bites.

©2001 Options Publishing, Inc.

7. **Spelling mistakes can ruin a good piece of writing. Circle the misspelled words in the sentences below. Some sentences have two mistakes.**

   a. Somtimes a vampire bat carrys rabies.

   b. You must aviod those bats at all costs.

   c. A special chemcial in bat spit can save humen lives.

   d. Scintists are studying this chemical closly.

8. ***This, that, these,* and *those* are demonstrative pronouns. *This* and *that* are singular. *These* and *those* are plural. Underline the correct pronoun in each of these sentences.**

   a. (This / That) bat in the tree over there seems to be sleeping.

   b. Look up! Do you see any bats in (these / those) branches overhead?

   c. Let me show you a picture of a bat. It's right here in (this / that) book.

   d. (These / Those) woods on that hill might have more bats.

9. **Commas should separate three or more words or phrases in a series. Place commas correctly in these sentences.**

   a. I learned about bats from books from television and from my uncle.

   b. Julie Kenneth and Samuel worked together on their report on bats.

   c. He saw bats in the barn last Monday Tuesday and Thursday.

10. **Underline the correct pronoun in each sentence.**

    a. Animals often do not realize that a bat bit (they / them).

    b. (They / Them) do not feel the bat's bite.

    c. If animals felt the bite, (they / them) would brush away the bat.

Writer's Tip

Are you using a computer to write your article? Use your computer spell-checker. Then check your article again. Spell-checkers miss many kinds of errors, such as using *if* instead of *it*.

Lesson 4: Editing

➤ **Now you are going to read and evaluate a persuasive article about coral reefs that April wrote. Her writing needs your help. Before you begin, read the checklist below.**

Writing Checklist

April will earn her best score if she meets these goals:

Ideas	• Excellent ideas
Order	• Ideas are in order
Sentences	• Sentences are easy to understand
Spelling and Punctuation	• No more than two mistakes

➤ These are the directions that April was given.

Directions: Write a persuasive article. Begin by stating a clear opinion. Then support your opinion with strong reasons. Explain your points in order. Put your strongest ideas last. End by repeating your opinion.

Rainforests of the Sea

(1) Coral reefs are called "rainforests of the sea." (2) About 5,000 kinds of fish live in the reefs. (3) Along with 2,500 kinds of coral. (4) Coral grows very slowly. (5) Some kinds grow only one-half inch a year. (6) It has taken thousands of years for reefs to form. (7) Every day, they are being damaged.

(8) Coral is a soft, tiny animal. (9) It cannot move around. (10) It gets it's food from the water. (11) Thousands of coral live close together. (12) They use the minerals to build shells around itself. (13) They take in minerals from the water.

(14) After the coral die, their shells remain. (15) New coral grow on these shells. (16) The shells are made from minerals. (17) The reef grows larger, layer by layer.

(18) Storms often damage reefs. (19) Strong waves can tear coral off the ocean floor. (20) We cannot stop storms. (21) But we can prevent other harm to reefs.

(22) For example, we can prevent damage from ships. (23) Ships crash into the reef. (24) They drop their anchors into them. (25) The anchors rip off chunks of coral.

(26) People take pieces of coral home. (27) You might have seen pieces of coral for sale. (28) In some places, explosives are used to break up the coral. (29) Then it is dragged out of the ocean. (30) The coral is crushed and used in building. (31) Some of it becomes fertilizer.

(32) Pollution also harms coral. (33) Oil spills kill the coral animals. (34) Fertilizers from farms and lawns poison them. (35) Soil from building sites washes into the ocean. (36) It covers the coral. (37) Dead coral loses its beautiful colors, it turns white.

(38) Reefs are not only beautiful. (39) They also protect beaches from strong waves. (40) They provide homes for millions of fish. (41) Some reef animals can be used for medicine.
(42) One of them is the sea slug.
(43) How many other reef
animals might help us?

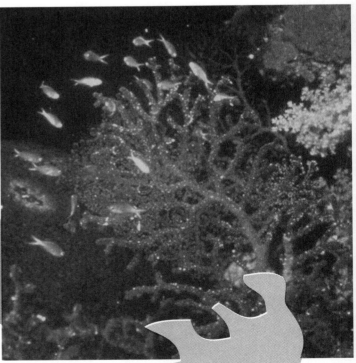

Now answer the following questions about April's article.

1. One of the first four sentences is a sentence fragment. Find it and rewrite it as a complete sentence.

   _____

   _____

2. Sentence 10 may have a misused word. How would you edit this word?

   Ⓐ their   Ⓒ it is

   Ⓑ its   Ⓓ no change needed

3. April used the wrong word in sentence 12. Which word below should be used instead?

   Ⓐ themself   Ⓒ themselves

   Ⓑ itsself   Ⓓ itselves

4. Sentence 12 is out of order. Which one of these sentences should it follow?

   Ⓐ sentence 8   Ⓒ sentence 13

   Ⓑ sentence 9   Ⓓ sentence 14

Writer's Tip

Remember apostrophes are used for contractions (*doesn't*) and possessive words (*the cat's tail* or *the boys' books*).

© 2001 Options Publishing, Inc.

5. Which of these sentences repeats information and should be taken out of the article?

Ⓐ sentence 14   Ⓒ sentence 16

Ⓑ sentence 15   Ⓓ sentence 17

6. Which sentence below is a run-on sentence?

Ⓐ sentence 29   Ⓒ sentence 37

Ⓑ sentence 34   Ⓓ sentence 40

7. April did not describe different kinds of coral. On the lines below, describe the coral in the pictures on pages 61 and 62.

Writer's Tip

When you describe something, consider how it looks, feels, sounds, smells, or even tastes.

_____

_____

_____

_____

8. Did April begin her article by stating a clear opinion? Does her first paragraph explain what she wants readers to do? Explain your answer.

_____

_____

_____

_____

9. Did April clearly describe how people are damaging coral reefs? Explain your answer.

_____

_____

_____

10. Did April place her reasons for protecting the reefs in a logical order? Explain your answer.

_____

_____

_____

11. April's article did not have a strong closing paragraph. Write a closing paragraph that will convince readers that her opinion is correct.

_____

_____

_____

_____

_____

_____

Writer's Tip

Persuade readers by choosing reasons that are important to them, such as their health as in April's article.

➤ **Here is a guide for evaluating writing. It is called a rubric. Use this rubric to evaluate April's article.**

Writing Rubric

Score	Ideas	Order	Sentences	Spelling and Punctuation
4	• Excellent ideas	• Ideas are in order	• Sentences are easy to understand	• No more than two mistakes
3	• Good ideas	• Most ideas are in order	• Most sentences are easy to understand	• No more than four mistakes
2	• Some ideas are not about the subject	• Some ideas are in order	• Some sentences are easy to understand	• No more than six mistakes
1	• Most ideas are not about the subject	• Few ideas are in order	• Few sentences are easy to understand	• No more than eight mistakes
0	• No work done	• No work done	• No work done	• No work done

➤ **Give April a score of 0 to 4 for each category. Explain why you gave her that score.**

Ideas _____

score

_____

_____

Order _____

score

_____

_____

Sentences_____

score

_____

_____

Spelling and Punctuation _____

score

_____

_____

➤ **Read the directions below. Then, read the checklist that you and your teacher will use to evaluate your writing.**

Directions: Now it's your turn to persuade readers to agree with you. First, think of something you strongly believe in. Then, think of reasons why you are correct. Begin your article by stating your opinion. Then, explain your reasons in order. Give examples of each reason. End by stating why your opinion is correct.

Writing Checklist

I will earn my best score if I achieve the following:

Ideas	• Excellent ideas
Order	• Ideas are in order
Sentences	• Sentences are easy to understand
Spelling and Punctuation	• No more than two mistakes

Plan Your Writing

➤ **Use these pages to plan your writing. You might find this graphic organizer helpful. If you need more room to write your first draft, use another sheet of paper.**

Opinion:
Reason 1:
Example:
Reason 2:
Example:
Reason 3:
Example:
Conclusion:

Writer's Tip

When you write an essay to persuade, make sure you state your opinion early. Then, state your reasons in logical order. Conclude the essay by restating your opinion.

_____

_____

_____

_____

_____

_____

Plan Your Writing

_____

_____

_____

_____

_____

Writer's Tip

Provide examples and facts to back up your opinion. You will be more likely to get readers to agree with you.

_____

_____

_____

_____

_____

_____

_____

_____

_____

_____

Writer's Tip

Here is a good way to think of ideas for an article. Start writing about your topic and do not stop for five minutes. Keep those ideas flowing. This is known as freewriting. Soon you will have many ideas for your article.

Writer's Tip

As you edit, look for words that do not add to your article or words that repeat what you have already explained. Delete those words.

Write Your Final Draft

➤ **Use all the skills you have learned in this unit to score well on a final draft. Remember to carefully proofread your work before you give it to your teacher.**

1 _____

2 _____

3 _____

4 _____

5 _____

6 _____

7 _____

8 _____

9 _____

10 _____

11 _____

12 _____

13 _____

14 _____

15 _____

16 _____

17 _____

18 _____

19 _____

20 _____

21 _____

22 _____

23 _____

24 _____

25 _____

26 _____

27 _____

28 _____

29 _____

30 _____

31 _____

32 _____

33 _____

Lesson 6: Your Turn to Write

➤ **Here is the same rubric you used to evaluate April's article. Now use it to evaluate your own persuasive article.**

Writing Rubric

Score	Ideas	Order	Sentences	Spelling and Punctuation
4	• Excellent ideas	• Ideas are in order	• Sentences are easy to understand	• No more than two mistakes
3	• Good ideas	• Most ideas are in order	• Most sentences are easy to understand	• No more than four mistakes
2	• Some ideas are not about the subject	• Some ideas are in order	• Some sentences are easy to understand	• No more than six mistakes
1	• Most ideas are not about the subject	• Few ideas are in order	• Few sentences are easy to understand	• No more than eight mistakes
0	• No work done	• No work done	• No work done	• No work done

➤ **Give your own writing a score of 0 to 4 for each category. Explain why you gave yourself that score.**

[ ] **Ideas** _____

score

_____

_____

[ ] **Order** _____

score

_____

_____

[ ] **Sentences** _____

score

_____

_____

[ ] **Spelling and Punctuation** _____

score

_____

_____

Think and Read

➤ **Do you like to listen to recorded music? Do you have tapes or compact discs (CDs)? How do you think music is recorded? Write your ideas on the lines below. Then read this article.**

_____

_____

Sounds Good!

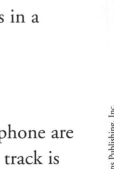

What if music could not be recorded? You would hear it only at concerts. Maybe you would have to listen to your family and friends sing! Lucky for us, music can be recorded to play on tapes and CDs.

Recording always starts with a microphone. Inside the microphone is a thin disc. Sound waves travel through the air. They push against this disc. The sound waves make the disc move. The microphone changes this movement into electric signals. These signals can then be stored on a CD or cassette tape. They each store the signals in a different way.

Recording CDs

CDs record using light. The electric signals from the microphone are sent to a laser light. The light burns a track into the CD. The track is made of shallow holes, called pits. Each song makes a track with a slightly different pattern of pits.

©2001 Options Publishing, Inc.

When you play a CD, the player shines a light on the track. It shines on one small area at a time. The pits reflect a pattern of light. The player changes that light pattern back into electrical signals. Those signals are sent to a speaker. The speaker changes the electric signals back into sound. Then you can hear your favorite music!

Recording Tapes

Cassette tapes record using magnetism. A tape is covered with tiny magnetic particles. The tape first moves past an erase head. This head makes sure the tape has no sound on it. Then the tape moves past a recording head. The recording head receives electric signals from the microphone. The head changes these signals into a magnetic pattern. It then moves the particles on the tape into this pattern. The sound is now stored in a magnetic pattern on the tape.

To play the tape, first rewind it. Then press *play*. The tape moves past a playback head. This head changes the magnetic pattern on the tape back into electric signals. These signals go to a speaker. The speaker changes them back into music.

Both kinds of recording begin with electric signals. The signals are changed into other kinds of patterns. We can change these patterns back into music. All we have to do is push a button on a CD or tape player. We can hear music whenever we wish!

Laser

The laser light shines on the pits in a CD. The pattern of light reflected back is changed to an electric signal.

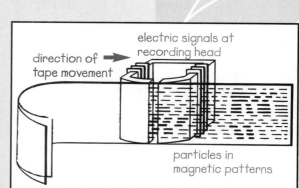

As the tape moves past the recording head, the electric signals are changed into a magnetic pattern on the tape.

direction of tape movement

electric signals at recording head

particles in magnetic patterns

Prewriting and Referencing

➤ **Monica's class was asked to write articles that explain recorded sound. To begin, Monica made a word web. She wrote questions about topics she could think of that were related to CDs. Use Monica's word web to answer questions 1-3.**

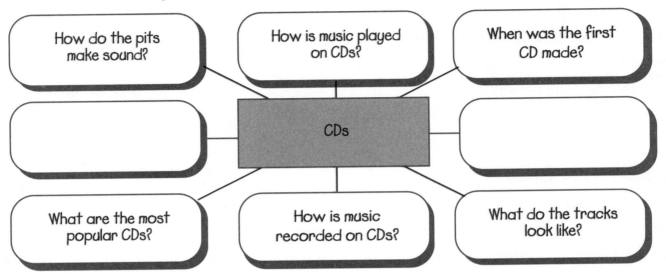

1. **Which idea would be the BEST addition to Monica's word web?**

   Ⓐ How much do CDs cost?

   Ⓑ Which entertainer has sold the most CDs?

   Ⓒ What are other uses of lasers?

   Ⓓ How do CDs compare with cassette tapes?

2. **Which idea from the web should Monica NOT use in her report?**

   Ⓐ How do the pits make sound?

   Ⓑ What do the tracks look like?

   Ⓒ What are the most popular CDs?

   Ⓓ How is music played on CDs?

3. **Monica's word web is not complete. What else could she find out about how CDs are made?**

   _____

   _____

➤ **Monica used an encyclopedia on CD-ROM to find information. She typed in the keyword *compact disc*. Below are some of the topics that Monica found. Use them to answer questions 4-6.**

FIND: COMPACT DISC

Items containing the words *compact disc*

 compact disc

Asia	laser
astronomy	inventions
computer	science fiction
copyright	sound recording
electric fish	television

Writer's Tip

Monica should have put her keyword in quotation marks, like this: *"compact disc."* Then the CD-ROM would have listed entries in which these two words appear one after the other.

4. **Which topic below is likely to show Monica how a CD works?**

   Ⓐ Asia

   Ⓑ compact disc

   Ⓒ electric fish

   Ⓓ television

5. **Which topic below is probably not related to CDs?**

   Ⓐ computer

   Ⓑ sound recording

   Ⓒ laser

   Ⓓ electric fish

6. **Review the questions in Monica's word web. Which topic below might be the BEST source of information for her report?**

   Ⓐ astronomy

   Ⓑ inventions

   Ⓒ copyright

   Ⓓ science fiction

Noodle Around

Writers use many resources when they research topics. What resources can Monica use? Talk about it with a friend.

©2001 Options Publishing, Inc.

➤ **Now check your answers. If you answered a question incorrectly, study the correct answer.**

1. **Which idea would be the BEST addition to Monica's word web?**

   Answer Ⓓ is the best answer. CDs and cassette tapes relate to the topic of recorded sound.

2. **Which idea from the web should Monica NOT use in her report?**

   Did you choose Answer Ⓒ? The most popular compact discs are constantly changing. Besides, this topic has little to do with how CDs are made.

3. **Monica's word web is not complete. What else could she find out about how CDs are made?**

   Your answer should relate to compact discs. For example:

   How are CDs similar to video discs? How are CDs similar to a cassette tape? How is a CD similar to a CD-ROM? Are compact discs used in digital video discs (DVDs)?

4. **Which topic below is likely to show Monica how a CD works?**

   Answer Ⓑ is correct. The movie camera picture means that the CD-ROM includes a short movie that shows how CDs work.

5. **Which topic below is probably not related to CDs?**

   Answer Ⓓ is correct. Monica's computer search looked for articles that had the words *compact* and *disc*. The entry for *electric fish* happens to include the words *compact nerve endings* and *discharges*.

6. **Review the questions in Monica's word web. Which topic below might be the BEST source of information for her report?**

   Did you choose Answer Ⓑ? It will tell Monica when and by whom CDs were invented.

► Here is a chance to work on your prewriting and referencing skills. Answer the questions on the next three pages.

1. It's important to learn quick ways to search for information. Enter each of these keywords into a word search on a CD-ROM encyclopedia in your classroom or school media ceter. Compare the lists of entries for each one.

   a. compact disc

   b. "compact disc"

   c. compact + disc

   d. compact and disc

   _____

   _____

   _____

2. When you are gathering information, use your time wisely. On page 79, review the list of items containing the words *compact disc*. List two topics you would try first. Explain your choices.

   _____

   _____

   _____

3. Word webs are one way to brainstorm ideas. Do you expect Monica's report to answer all the questions in her web? Why or why not?

   _____

   _____

4. Accuracy is important. Monica saw a TV show several weeks ago about making CDs. She thinks she'll write what she remembers as best as she can for her report. Do you think her memory of the show will give accurate information? Why or why not?

_____

_____

_____

5. When doing research, check that your sources have the most up-to-date information. Which of the following sources would have the most up-to-date information?

Ⓐ a magazine published in 1999

Ⓑ a book published in 1999

Ⓒ the Internet

Ⓓ a CD-ROM encyclopedia produced in 2000

6. Should Monica write her outline before or after she does her research? Explain your answer.

_____

_____

_____

_____

_____

7. Writing an informative report involves making some decisions. As Monica writes her outline, should she try to include every fact she found? Why or why not?

_____

_____

_____

8. Be ready to solve problems as you write. In the encyclopedia articles, Monica came across some terms such as *polycarbonate plastic substrate*. She does not know what this term means, so she could not understand the article. What should she do?

_____

_____

_____

_____

Writer's Tip

When you research, only write down facts you understand. Use a dictionary to help you with words you don't know.

9. When prewriting, authors must decide on their purpose for writing. Write a sentence telling Monica's purpose for writing her article.

_____

_____

_____

_____

► **Read this part of Monica's rough draft. Then answer questions 1-6.**

CDs Are the Pits!

(1) Today, most music is recorded on CDs.
(2) You might have some CDs of your own.
(3) I have more than ten of them.
(4) In this report, you will learn how music is recorded in this report on CDs. (5) You might be surprised at how it's done! (6) Then you will learn how CDs are different from tapes.
(7) You will also find out how CDs play music.

(8) The master CD starts out smooth, flat, and shiny. (9) As this CD spins, the laser beam -on its bottom side burns a track. (10) The track is actually a pattern of shallow holls or pits that are so small you cannot see them. (11) You would need a microscope to see them. (12) Recordings are made on a master CD.

1. **Rewrite sentence 4 so that it doesn't repeat information.**

_____

_____

_____

_____

2. Sentence 7 is not in the correct order. Which of the sentences below should sentence 7 best FOLLOW?

Ⓐ sentence 1   Ⓒ sentence 5

Ⓑ sentence 2   Ⓓ sentence 8

3. Which sentence below should be deleted from this report?

Ⓐ sentence 1   Ⓒ sentence 3

Ⓑ sentence 2   Ⓓ sentence 4

4. Sentence 9 is poorly written. Rewrite it using correct grammar.

_____

_____

_____

Writer's Tip

It's important to write clearly. For example, Monica first explains how music is recorded on CDs. In the next part of her draft, she will explain how CDs produce music. She describes each step in chronological order.

5. Which sentence below does not add to the story?

Ⓐ sentence 8   Ⓒ sentence 10

Ⓑ sentence 9   Ⓓ sentence 11

6. Sentence 12 is out of order. Which of these sentences should it come BEFORE?

Ⓐ sentence 1   Ⓒ sentence 8

Ⓑ sentence 5   Ⓓ sentence 11

Noodle Around

Sometimes, a rough draft will contain redundant or repeated information. Which question asks you about redundant information? Discuss your answer with a partner.

Lesson 3: Composing and Revising

➤ **Now check your answers. If you answered a question incorrectly, study the correct answer.**

1. **Rewite sentence 4 so that it doesn't repeat information. The sentence should be rewritten as follows:**

   In this report, you will learn how music is recorded on CDs.

2. **Sentence 7 is not in the correct order. Which of the sentences below should sentence 7 best FOLLOW?**

   Answer Ⓒ is correct. Sentences 4 and 5 talk about recording music. It makes sense to put sentence 7 next because it talks about playing music.

3. **Which sentence below should be taken out of this report?**

   Did you choose Answer Ⓒ? Sentence 3 does not add any important information to this report.

4. **Sentence 9 is poorly written. Rewrite it using correct grammar.**

   Prepositional phrases should be placed as close as possible to the words they describe. *On its bottom side* describes the track, not the beam. Here is a clearer rewrite of the sentence:

   As this CD spins, the laser beam burns a track on its bottom side.

5. **Which sentence below does not add to the story?**

   Answer Ⓓ is the correct answer. Sentence 11 is not necessary because it just repeats the idea that the pits are tiny.

6. **Sentence 12 is out of order. Which of these sentences should it come BEFORE?**

   Answer Ⓒ is correct. Sentence 12 is the topic sentence for the second paragraph.

Try It

> Here is a chance to work on your composing and revising skills. Answer the questions on the next three pages.

1. **Every sentence in a paragraph should support the paragraph topic. Should Monica include either sentence below in her first paragraph? Explain your answer.**

   Most people don't know how CDs work, but they play them anyway.

   _____

   _____

   A CD track is thinner than a human hair.

   _____

   _____

2. **Make sure the information you are sharing is correct. Based on the article you read on pages 76-77, which sentences below are accurate? Mark each one *T* for true or *F* for false.**

   a. _____ The tracks on CDs are called lasers.

   b. _____ The microphone sends electric signals to a laser machine.

   c. _____ The laser records magnetic patterns on the disc.

Lesson 3: Composing and Revising

3. **Be sure to place words in order when you write sentences. Improve these sentences by rewriting them.**

On a very small area of the track, a lens focuses the laser beam.

_____

_____

When the laser bounces off the pits, of light a pattern it produces.

_____

_____

4. **Paragraphs should begin with a sentence that introduces the topic. Does the second paragraph in Monica's article begin with a good topic sentence? Explain your answer.**

_____

_____

_____

5. **Did Monica choose a good title for her report? Explain your answer.**

_____

_____

_____

_____

6. Writers should not confuse readers with too much detail. Which of the sentences below should Monica include in her report? Explain your answer.

Ⓐ CDs can also record photographs and video.

Ⓑ A CD is 4.75 in (12.07 cm) in diameter.

Ⓒ CDs were invented by James T. Russell.

_____

_____

Writer's Tip

When you revise your writing, look for things you really like about it first. It is a good way to get started. Then, look for things you could improve.

7. Writers must explain their ideas in a logical order. The sentences below are out of order. Number them from 1 to 4 based on how they appear in the article.

a. _____ The light burns a track into the disc.

b. _____ The microphone sends the electric signals to the CD recorder.

c. _____ Sound waves reach the microphone and are changed into electric signals.

d. _____ The electric signals control a laser light in the recorder.

8. Try to avoid short, choppy sentences. Combine each set of short sentences below into one longer sentence.

The laser shines on the disc. The laser burns a track into the disc.

_____

_____

Protect the bottom of your CDs. That is where the music is recorded.

_____

_____

Lesson 3: Composing and Revising

▶ **Now read the rest of Monica's rough draft. This section has groups of underlined words. Editing questions will be asked about them.**

(13) This master CD is used to make copies that are <u>selled</u> in stores. (14) To play a CD, slip it into a CD player. (15) The player spins the CD around <u>real fast</u>. (16) As it spins the CD, the player points a weak laser light at a spot on the track.

(17) <u>A scanner in the player read</u> this pattern of light. (18) Then the player changes the light pattern back into electric signals. (19) A speaker in the player turns the signals back into your favorite music.

(20) CDs are different from tapes in several ways. (21) <u>CDs can store much more music, than a tape.</u> (22) The music from a CD also sounds more like the <u>orginal</u> music. (23) Finally, CDs do not wear out. (24) <u>Nothing but light never touches them</u> while they play.

(25) Now that you know how CDs work, why dont you listen to your favorite group.

1. **How should Monica edit the underlined part of sentence 13? Rewrite the sentence for her.**

   _____

   _____

2. **How should Monica edit the underlined part of sentence 15?**

   Ⓐ real fastly   Ⓒ fastest

   Ⓑ very fast   Ⓓ no change needed

3. How should Monica edit the underlined words in sentence 17? Rewrite the sentence correctly.

_____

_____

4. How should Monica edit sentence 21?

Ⓐ CDs can store much, more music than a tape.

Ⓑ CDs can store much more music than a tape.

Ⓒ CDs can store much-more music than a tape.

Ⓓ no change needed

5. Rewrite sentence 22. Correct the spelling of the underlined word.

_____

_____

6. How should Monica edit the underlined part of sentence 24?

Ⓐ No light never touches them

Ⓑ Nothing but light ever touches them

Ⓒ No light ever touches them

Ⓓ no change needed

Writer's Tip

Most computers have a grammar checker that will catch some mistakes. But grammar checkers can make errors. Decide for yourself whether a change is needed.

Noodle Around

Past-tense verbs tell about action that has already happened. Which question asks you about a past-tense verb? Discuss your answer with a friend.

Lesson 4: Editing

➤ **Now check your answers. If you answered a question incorrectly, study the correct answer.**

1. **How should Monica edit the underlined part of sentence 13? Rewrite the sentence for her.**

   The past tense of *sell* is *sold*. Here is the correct rewrite:

   This master CD is used to make copies that are <u>sold</u> in stores.

2. **How should Monica edit the underlined part of sentence 15?**

   Answer Ⓑ is correct. Monica needs the adverb *very* here, telling "how fast."

3. **How should Monica edit the underlined words in sentence 17?**

   The corrected sentence is below. The verb *reads* should be singular to match the singular subject, *scanner*. For example:

   A scanner in the player reads this pattern of light.

4. **How should Monica edit sentence 21?**

   Answer Ⓑ is correct. This sentence does not need a comma or a hyphen.

5. **Rewrite sentence 22. Correct the spelling of the underlined word.**

   The sentence should be rewritten as follows:

   The music from a CD also sounds more like the original music.

6. **How should Monica edit the underlined part of sentence 24?**

   Did you choose Answer Ⓑ? It has only one negative word: *nothing*. Answer Ⓐ has two negative words.

Try It

➤ **Here is a chance to work on your editing skills. Answer the questions on the next three pages.**

1. Irregular verbs do not form their past tense by adding *-ed.* Write the past tense of these irregular verbs.

   a. ride _____   **d.** know _____

   b. speak _____   **e.** fall _____

   c. sleep _____   **f.** become _____

2. *Real* and *good* are adjectives because they describe nouns. *Really* and *very* are adverbs, which can describe verbs, adjectives, or other adverbs. Circle the correct adjective or adverb in each sentence below.

   a. The game was (real / really) good.

   b. The score was (real / very) close.

   c. Our team was a (real / really) success.

3. Never use two negatives in one sentence. Beside each sentence below, write *C* for correct or *I* for incorrect. If it is incorrect, rewrite the sentence on the lines below.

   a. _____ No one never listens to too much music.

   b. _____ That store does not have the ones I like.

   c. _____ I don't have none by that singer.

   _____

   _____

   _____

Lesson 4: Editing

4. **Before you add a question mark, make sure the sentence really asks a question. Add the correct ending punctuation to these sentences.**

   a. She asked me if I had that CD _____

   b. Where did you buy that one _____

   c. I wondered if that was his sister's CD _____

5. **The past tense of irregular verbs is not formed by adding *-ed*. Circle the correct spelling in each sentence below.**

   a. CDs are (maked / made) with laser lights.

   b. Yesterday I (took / taked) a good look at the bottom of a CD.

   c. I (finded / found) that I could not see a track on the CD.

   d. Still, I (knew / knowed) the track was there.

6. **Subjects and verbs must agree. Check the subject-verb agreement in these sentences. Write *C* for correct and *I* for incorrect next to each sentence.**

   a. _____ The CDs in that stack is my favorites.

   b. _____ The newest CD from that group is on sale now.

   c. _____ My friends at school shares CDs.

   d. _____ The speaker in my CD player is broken.

7. **Good writers check their spelling carefully. Find and circle the misspelled word in each sentence below.**

   a. Did you ever see someone use a lazer pointer?

   b. Lasers are also used in hospitals to do sergery.

   c. The laser light does not ware out the CD.

   d. When you listen to music, do you perfer tapes or CDs?

8. A sentence should have no more than one negative word. Write *C* for correct or *I* for incorrect. Rewrite each incorrect sentence on the lines below.

a. _____ I haven't never heard that CD before.

b. _____ None of my friends has ever heard it.

c. _____ I haven't ever heard nothing like it.

_____

_____

9. Often you can turn an adjective into an adverb by adding *-ly*. Circle the correct word in each sentence below.

a. Can you hear the music (clear / clearly)?

b. It is not playing (real / really) loud.

c. Be (careful / carefully) when you handle a CD.

d. The music is playing (quiet / quietly) now.

10. The apostrophe in a contraction shows that letters have been left out. Write the contractions for these words below.

a. could not _____

b. it is _____

c. is not _____

d. will not _____

e. we are _____

f. they have _____

Writer's Tip

A thesaurus lists synonyms for words. It can help you choose exactly the right word for a certain sentence. For example, synonyms for *run* include *flee, melt, flow, speed, operate,* and *direct*.

Lesson 4: Editing

➤ **Read and evaluate an informative report that Nicholas wrote about how famous singers and musicians make CDs. His writing needs your help. Before you start, read the checklist below.**

Writing Checklist

Nicholas will earn his best score if he meets these goals:

Ideas	• Excellent ideas
Order	• Ideas are in order
Sentences	• Sentences are easy to understand
Spelling and Punctuation	• No more than two mistakes

➤ **These are the directions that Nicholas was given.**

Directions: Write an informative report about recording music or sound. Research your topic thoroughly. Then, organize your points in order. Think of a strong beginning, middle, and end for your report.

Mixing up a CD

(1) Recording a CD is not easy! (2) The producer is in charge. (3) Many other people also help make the CD. (4) This person makes the important decisions.

(5) The CD is recorded in a studio. (6) Most studioes have two rooms. (7) One room is for the performers. (8) It must be very quiet. (9) There must be no sound accept for the performers. (10) Microphones are spread around this room. (11) Each singer has one. (12) Each instrument has one.

(13) The studio also has a control room. (14) That's where the engineers work. (15) They can see the performers through a window.

(16) Before a CD is made, the recording equipment is checked. (17) It perfectly must be working. (18) Then the performers sing or play. (19) They might have to repeat a song many times. (20) The sound from each microphone is recorded on its own sound track.

Lesson 5: Evaluate Writing

(21) The performers often wear headphones. (22) The headphones help them here themself. (23) They can also hear directions from the producer. (24) The producer stays in the control room.

(25) After the song is recorded, the mix engineer gets to work. (26) This person listens to each sound track and to all the sound tracks playing together. (27) If one guitar is too loud, the engineer turns that sound track down.

(28) If one singer is too soft, that sound track is turned up.
(29) The engineer can make sounds louder or softer. (30) The engineer can also change the sounds in other ways. (31) Some sounds might not even be used.

(32) Next, a mastering engineer makes more small changes. (33) This person helps make the CD sound great. (34) Finally, the CD is sent to the company that makes it and prints the label.

(35) When you buy a CD, you buy the work of many people. (36) Not all of their names are on the CD.

©2001 Options Publishing, Inc.

1. **Sentence 4 is in the wrong place. Which sentence should it follow?**

   Ⓐ sentence 1

   Ⓑ sentence 2

   Ⓒ sentence 5

   Ⓓ sentence 6

2. **Sentence 6 has a misspelled or misused word. Which word below should replace it?**

   Ⓐ More

   Ⓑ studios

   Ⓒ too

   Ⓓ no change needed

Writer's Tip

Part of being a good writer is knowing which words are hard for you. If words, such as *except* and *accept*, confuse you, be sure to learn the difference. Then, you will not use them incorrectly.

3. **Sentence 9 has a misused word. How would you edit this word?**

   Ⓐ except

   Ⓑ excerpt

   Ⓒ excess

   Ⓓ no change needed

4. **Nicholas decided to combine sentences 11 and 12. Write one good way to combine them.**

   _____

   _____

5. Sentence 17 is poorly written. Which of these sentences should Nicholas use instead?

Ⓐ Perfectly, it must be working.

Ⓑ It must be perfectly working.

Ⓒ It must be working perfectly.

Ⓓ no change needed

6. Sentence 22 has two mistakes in it. Rewite the sentence correctly below.

_____

_____

7. Which of these sentences repeats something Nicholas has already explained?

Ⓐ sentence 26   Ⓒ sentence 28

Ⓑ sentence 27   Ⓓ sentence 29

8. Sentence 34 is poorly written. How should Nicholas edit it?

Ⓐ Finally, the CD is printed.

Ⓑ Finally, the CD's label is printed.

Ⓒ Finally, the CD's label is printing.

Ⓓ no change needed

Writer's Tip

Read your work aloud to help find difficult sentences. Find someone to read your work aloud, too.

©2001 Options Publishing, Inc.

9. Does Nicholas' article have a strong beginning? Does it introduce the topic and grab readers' interest? Explain your answer.

_____

_____

_____

10. Did Nicholas discuss his points in order? Explain your answer.

_____

_____

_____

11. Nicholas' article did not have a strong closing paragraph. Write a closing sentence that describes how CDs are recorded.

_____

_____

_____

_____

_____

_____

Writer's Tip

In an informative article, the closing paragraph often restates the main points.

Lesson 5: Evaluate Writing

➤ **Here is a rubric, a guide for evaluating writing. Use this rubric to evaluate Nicholas' report.**

Writing Rubric

Score	Ideas	Order	Sentences	Spelling and Punctuation
4	• Excellent ideas	• Ideas are in order	• Sentences are easy to understand	• No more than two mistakes
3	• Good ideas	• Most ideas are in order	• Most sentences are easy to understand	• No more than four mistakes
2	• Some ideas are not about the subject	• Some ideas are in order	• Some sentences are easy to understand	• No more than six mistakes
1	• Most ideas are not about the subject	• Few ideas are in order	• Few sentences are easy to understand	• No more than eight mistakes
0	• No work done	• No work done	• No work done	• No work done

➤ **Give Nicholas a score of 0 to 4 for each category. Explain why you gave him that score.**

☐
score

Ideas _____

_____

_____

☐
score

Order _____

_____

_____

☐
score

Sentences _____

_____

_____

☐
score

Spelling and Punctuation _____

_____

_____

➤ **Read the directions below. Then, read the checklist that you and your teacher will use to evaluate your writing.**

Directions: Choose a topic that relates to music and interests you. First, think of possible ideas. Then, learn more about your topic. Put the facts and ideas you gather into an outline. Organize your points in order. Then, write a strong beginning, middle, and end.

Writing Checklist

I will earn my best score if I achieve the following:

Ideas	• Excellent ideas
Order	• Ideas are in order
Sentences	• Sentences are easy to understand
Spelling and Punctuation	• No more than two mistakes

©2001 Options Publishing, Inc.

Plan Your Writing

➤ **Use these pages to plan your writing. You might find this graphic organizer helpful.**

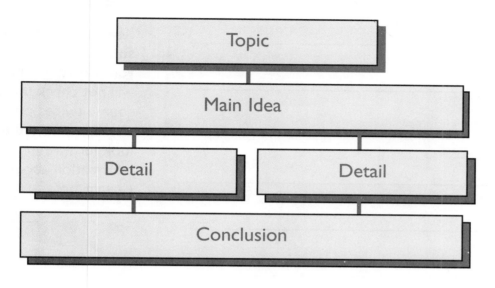

Writer's Tip

The more planning you do now, the less revising you will have to do later.

_____

_____

_____

_____

_____

_____

_____

_____

Plan Your Writing

©2001 Options Publishing, Inc.

© 2001 Options Publishing, Inc.

Writer's Tip

Look at your article from your reader's point of view. Have you answered the main questions a reader might have about this topic?

Writer's Tip

A good title will catch your readers' attention. Headings for each section will help organize your ideas. Headings will also tell readers what to expect when they read that section.

Lesson 6: Your Turn to Write

Write Your Final Draft

➤ **Use all the skills you have learned in this unit to score well on a final draft. Remember to carefully proofread your work before you give it to your teacher.**

1 _____

2 _____

3 _____

4 _____

5 _____

6 _____

7 _____

8 _____

9 _____

10 _____

11 _____

12 _____

13 _____

14 _____

15 _____

16 _____

17 _____

18 _____

19 _____

20 _____

21 _____

22 _____

23 _____

24 _____

25 _____

26 _____

27 _____

28 _____

29 _____

30 _____

31 _____

32 _____

33 _____

Lesson 6: Your Turn to Write

➤ **Here is the same rubric you used to evaluate Nicholas' report. Use it to evaluate your own report.**

Writing Rubric

Score	Ideas	Order	Sentences	Spelling and Punctuation
4	• Excellent ideas	• Ideas are in order	• Sentences are easy to understand	• No more than two mistakes
3	• Good ideas	• Most ideas are in order	• Most sentences are easy to understand	• No more than four mistakes
2	• Some ideas are not about the subject	• Some ideas are in order	• Some sentences are easy to understand	• No more than six mistakes
1	• Most ideas are not about the subject	• Few ideas are in order	• Few sentences are easy to understand	• No more than eight mistakes
0	• No work done	• No work done	• No work done	• No work done

> **Give your writing a score of 0 to 4 for each category. Explain why you gave yourself that score.**

☐
score

Ideas _____

_____

_____

☐
score

Order _____

_____

_____

☐
score

Sentences _____

_____

_____

☐
score

Spelling and Punctuation _____

_____

_____

Helpful Tips

Editing Symbols		Examples
⊙	Insert a period	We went to the beach⊙ I found lots of shells.
⋏	Insert a comma	Our friend, Tawanda‸is having a party.
⋀	Insert a letter, word, phrase, or sentence	very It is‸cold outside.
℘	Take out a letter, word, or phrase	We want ice cream ~~today~~ for dessert.
☰	Change a lower-case letter to a capital letter	I saw mrs. file yesterday. ☰ ☰
/	Change a capital letter to a lower-case letter	We are going to the M̸ovies tonight.
SP	Check the spelling of the word	ⓈⓅ My litle brother is coming with us.

Use the correct punctuation mark at the end of every sentence	
Use a period for a statement or command:	I brought my lunch today.
Use a question mark for a question:	What is in your lunch?
Use an exclamation point for a sentence with feeling:	That is my favorite movie!
Use a comma	
between words in a list:	I have a dog, a cat, and a goldfish.
between two short sentences:	I was almost late, but I got there.
Use an apostrophe	
in contractions:	didn't (did not); I'm (I am)
in words that show ownership:	dog's tail; girls' team